A souvenir guide

Virginia Woolf at Monk's House

East Sussex

Claire Masset

❀ National Trust

'An unpretending house'

A simple cottage of no real pretension, Monk's House suited Virginia and Leonard Woolf perfectly.

'There is little ceremony or precision at Monks House. It is an unpretending house,' Virginia noted in her diary after her first visit. 'These rooms are small, I said to myself… The kitchen is distinctly bad. There's an oil stove, & no grate. Nor is there hot water, nor a bath.'

This primitive cottage on the edge of the East Sussex village of Rodmell was far from ideal, but it didn't matter. Cautiously, Virginia kept 'excitement at bay', but she had already fallen in love with the place. When her husband Leonard saw the garden, with its 'infinity of fruitbearing trees', its promising outbuildings and its proximity to meadows and long walks, the decision was made. Virginia declared it to be 'ours'.

The perfect retreat

The year was 1919. Virginia was 37, Leonard 39. They had been married for seven years. Monk's House would be their country retreat – a weekend home where they could read, write, garden and go for long walks. 'Monks House…will be our address for ever and ever,' Virginia wrote to her friend Ka Arnold-Forster in August. 'Indeed, I've already marked out our graves in the yard which joins our meadow.' Over the years, they spent their earnings renovating and extending the house, slowly increasing its comforts until it became a more permanent base.

It was here that Virginia wrote many of her bestselling books, such as *Mrs Dalloway* (1925), *To the Lighthouse* (1927), *Orlando* (1928) and *The Waves* (1931). In the quietness and solitude of the South Downs, which she adored, she found peace, solace and moments of real happiness in a life punctuated by episodes of crippling depression and anxiety. In 1930, she described what Monk's House brought her: 'How happy I am: how calm, for the moment how sweet life is with L here, in its regularity & order, & the garden & the room at night & music & my walks & writing easily & interestedly.'

A creative couple

Monk's House is filled with Virginia's presence. You sense it in her bedroom where her shawl lies draped on the armchair, in the piles of books left on every possible surface, and in the writing shed at the bottom of the garden, where her little round glasses rest on the desk.

But this was also Leonard's house. He was not just a constant support for his talented yet troubled wife, but a successful publisher, civil servant, political theorist and writer. To him we also owe the wonderful garden. This was his passion, which he carried on pursuing for another 28 years after Virginia's tragic suicide in 1941.

Left Monk's House, as seen from the road in Rodmell

'Who was I then?'

Virginia asks this question in *A Sketch of the Past,* her unfinished autobiographical memoir.

'Adeline Virginia Stephen,' she continues, 'the second daughter of Leslie and Julia Prinsep Stephen, born on 25 January 1882, descended from a great many people, some famous, others obscure; born not of rich parents but of well-to-do parents, born into a very communicative, literate letter-writing, visiting, articulate, late nineteenth-century world…'

Virginia Woolf (1882–1941) was born in the Victorian age but she emerged an adult at the dawn of the 20th century. A fearless and godless era was beginning: a world of speed and freedom, of radical questioning and new ways of seeing, of motor cars and planes, of female emancipation and psychoanalysis, war and destruction.

Virginia was acutely conscious of her role in these changing times. 'I shall reform the novel,' she wrote as early as 1908. Her life became a quest to discover a new form of writing. Her novels portrayed life and the workings of the mind through a deeper, more fluid and sophisticated prism and reflected the complex and unstable world in which she lived. Impressions, pictures, thoughts and sensations were conveyed in a swirling 'stream of consciousness' replacing old-fashioned conventions of character, plot and time.

Portrait of a writer

Virginia's profile was famously caught on camera by George Charles Beresford when she was just 20 years old. Here was an attractive pale-skinned woman lost in thought, with a long delicate face, inquisitive eyes, well-defined lips and a Grecian nose. Despite her attractiveness, Virginia hated being captured in photography and paint. What mattered to her was the life of the mind. Above all Virginia Woolf is a voice. Her works possess an intimacy that makes you feel you know her. 'I sometimes think only autobiography is literature – novels are what we peel off, and come at last to the core, which is only you or me,' Virginia wrote in a letter in 1932.

Her output was varied and prolific. She penned thousands of letters, committed her thoughts and activities to her diary, wrote essays and literary criticism, short stories, and longer works of fiction, for which she is best known.

Throughout this tireless working life, she dealt with long periods of depression, often unable to eat, sleep, read or write, suffering delusions and severe symptoms of anxiety. Despite her self-inflicted death at the relatively young age of 59, she lived a full life with deep friendships and a happy marriage. She was a central figure in the Bloomsbury Group. She was a publisher, a lecturer, a reviewer and a feminist. And she was one of the great thinkers of her time. Perhaps her most appealing trait is that she was intensely human. Flawed, self-doubting, honest, brave and always questioning, she is one of us.

Right This photograph by George Charles Beresford, taken in 1902, shows a young contemplative Virginia

'The little sealed loop'

Virginia grew up in an intellectual and artistic household. Her father Leslie, editor of the monumental *Dictionary of National Biography*, enjoyed considerable standing in the literary world. Her mother Julia had been a Pre-Raphaelite model, whose aunt was the famous photographer Julia Margaret Cameron.

Both widowed, with children from previous marriages, Leslie and Julia had four children together: Vanessa, Thoby, Virginia and Adrian. The narrow six-storey family home at 22 Hyde Park Gate in Kensington was dark and claustrophobic. Crowded with up to 17 other people, it was further peopled with endless rounds of visitors. In 'the little sealed loop' of Hyde Park Gate, 'everybody knew everybody, and everything about everybody', Virginia wrote in *A Sketch of the Past*, recalling her feeling of confinement.

Below left Sir Leslie Stephen, in a photograph by John Caswall Smith from the 1890s

Below A young and beautiful Julia Stephen, photographed by her aunt Julia Margaret Cameron, 1867

Right Virginia with her mother and father photographed in 1893 while holidaying in St Ives, where the Stephen family spent many summers (see page 46)

Bottom right Produced by Virginia and her sister Vanessa, the *Hyde Park Gate News* was a family 'newspaper' filled with stories, poems, drawings, fictional letters and even plays. It was the perfect training ground for a budding writer and fledgling artist

A home education

Further constriction was endured because of her sex. Like other middle-class girls, Virginia and her older sister Vanessa were educated at home, while Thoby and Adrian went to boarding school. Leslie taught his daughters maths and classics and gave them access to his extensive library. Virginia devoured his books and, with few friends of her own age, relied on Vanessa for company. They would be confidantes all their lives. Despite spending much of his time in his upstairs study, Leslie could be an attentive father. He read to his children, told them stories and caught moths and butterflies with them. Throughout her life, Virginia would have a strange fascination for 'that old wretch my father'. More than any of his other children, Virginia understood him. Their shared love of books and writing, and his belief in her ability as a writer, further cemented their connection.

Her mother Julia was a more distant figure. When she wasn't busy running the house or performing social duties, she visited the sick in London's hospitals and workhouses. She encapsulated the Victorian ideal of womanhood: the 'angel in the house', selfless, almost saintly. She would always remain a mystery to Virginia.

First steps in storytelling

From the confines of their nursery, Virginia and Vanessa enjoyed making up tales about their neighbours. Further testing their creative powers, from 1892 they wrote and illustrated a weekly newspaper, the *Hyde Park Gate News*, all about life in the family home. Aged 10, Virginia was already a writer and a publisher.

Early losses

Virginia's childhood came to a halt when her mother died unexpectedly, aged 49, in May 1895. Virginia was just 13. Shocked at her own reaction, Virginia felt nothing, but the numbness soon turned into the first of her breakdowns. After two years she surfaced from her depression, only to lose her half-sister Stella Duckworth. The final hammer blow to her youth was the death of her father, from cancer, in 1904.

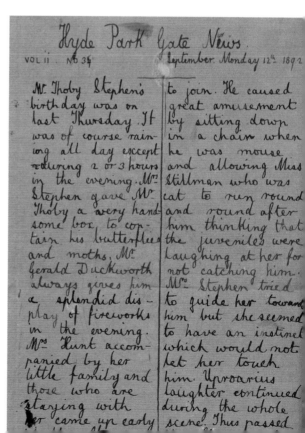

Hyde Park Gate News.

VOL II Nᵒ 35 September. Monday 12ᵗʰ 1892

'Experiments in living'

With no father to care for, the Stephen children were free to leave the family home and start afresh. Vanessa searched for a place that would be as different from bourgeois Kensington as possible. She found it in shabby, faded Bloomsbury. Bright and airy, the house at 46 Gordon Square was, according to Virginia, 'the most beautiful, the most exciting, the most romantic place in the world'.

Life for the siblings would never be the same again. 'Everything was going to be new; everything was going to be different. Everything was on trial,' wrote Virginia in her posthumously published collection of essays, *Moments of Being*. 'We were full of experiments and reforms. We were going to do without table napkins… we were going to paint; to write; to have coffee after dinner instead of tea at nine o'clock,' she continued.

Vanessa decorated the walls in light shades and draped Indian shawls over the furniture, creating relaxed room settings that would inspire a new style of interior design. Virginia settled into her new room, with her desk, typewriter and piles of books. The sisters could now devote themselves to their respective passions: painting and writing.

The Bloomsbury Group

A few months after moving in, Thoby started his Thursday 'at homes', inviting friends he had known at Cambridge for informal evenings of discussion. At first cautious and coy, Virginia quickly became a confident participant, revelling in this new outlet for expression. This was the start of the Bloomsbury Group: a close network of friends who shared a love of honesty, beauty and friendship. They valued freedom above all else and embarked on 'experiments in living' –

Above Thoby Stephen photographed by George Charles Beresford in 1906, the year of his death

Left Brown plaque commemorating the Bloomsbury Group inhabitants at 46 Gordon Square

Opposite Bloomsbury group members (left to right) Ottoline Morrell, Maria Huxley, Lytton Strachey, Duncan Grant and Vanessa Bell at Garsington Manor, Oxfordshire, in 1915. Home to Lady Ottoline, this Tudor house was a haven for intellectual gatherings, especially during the First World War, when conscientious objectors – many of them 'Bloomsberries' – came here to work on the home farm and discuss ideas

ERECTED BY CAMDEN LONDON BOROUGH COUNCIL
HERE AND IN NEIGHBOURING HOUSES DURING THE FIRST HALF OF THE 20th CENTURY THERE LIVED SEVERAL MEMBERS OF THE BLOOMSBURY GROUP INCLUDING VIRGINIA WOOLF CLIVE BELL AND THE STRACHEYS

so much so that the group became famous for its complicated love affairs. Amongst its members were the biographer Lytton Strachey, art critic Clive Bell, artists Roger Fry and Duncan Grant, novelist E.M. Forster and economist John Maynard Keynes.

Life in squares

Life in Bloomsbury did not stand still for long. In 1906, Thoby contracted typhoid while on holiday in Greece and died on his return to England. Two days after his death, Vanessa accepted Clive Bell's proposal of marriage. The couple stayed at Gordon Square, while Adrian and Virginia moved to Fitzroy Square, 10 minutes' walk away. In 1911, she and Adrian moved again, this time to

Brunswick Square. Defying Victorian propriety, Virginia shared the house with four men: her brother Adrian, John Maynard Keynes, Duncan Grant and, another of Thoby's Cambridge friends, Leonard Woolf, who rented the cheaper rooms upstairs. This 'penniless Jew' would soon fall in love with her.

Becoming a writer
Virginia's Bloomsbury years saw the start of her career. She began writing reviews for literary journals and blossomed into a confident journalist. 'My real delight in reviewing is to say nasty things,' she crowed in a letter to her friend Madge Vaughan in December 1904.

'A penniless Jew'

In the domestic setting of Brunswick Square, Leonard Woolf (1880–1969) became Virginia's friend. She soon felt comfortable enough to share her writing with him. At the time this slim, good-looking young man was taking a year off from his civil service job in Ceylon.

'He spent seven years in Ceylon, governing natives, inventing ploughs, shooting tigers,' Virginia wrote to her friend Madge Vaughan in June 1912. Leonard's exoticism, or at least his separateness (it was Virginia who famously described him as a 'penniless Jew'), may have been a source of attraction. What is certain is that their relationship was based on mutual respect and understanding. Leonard, she came to realise, was 'the one person to talk to'.

A proposal

When Leonard proposed in January 1912, Virginia had already had four offers of marriage from other suitors. She felt reluctant and nervous, unsure of her feelings. Ever the analyst, she weighed up the pros and cons. On 1 May, in one of her most candid letters, she wrote to Leonard: 'I pass from hot to cold in an instant, without any reason… All I can say is that in spite of those feelings which go chasing each other all day long when I am with you, there is some feeling which is permanent, and growing… I feel that I must

Opposite Virginia and Leonard in July 1912, shortly before their wedding in August of that year

give you everything; and that if I can't, well, marriage would only be second-best for you as well as for me… We both of us want a marriage that is a tremendous living thing, always alive, always hot, not dead and easy in parts as most marriages are. We ask a great deal of life, don't we? Perhaps we shall get it; then how splendid!'

Proving Virginia's bond to Leonard, the letter became a kind of manifesto for their life together. The couple married in St Pancras Town Hall on 10 August 1912.

Shared ambitions

Leaving his job in Ceylon, Leonard embarked on a successful career that would cover politics, journalism, writing, editing and publishing. Leonard and Virginia were equally devoted to work. During their married life, they rarely took a day off willingly.

Pet names
As a child Virginia and her siblings gave each other animal nicknames. Vanessa was alternately Dolphin, Sheepdog and Marmot. Virginia was known as Billy, Goat and Ape. The habit continued in adult life: Leonard become Mongoose, while he called Virginia, Mandrill.

Leonard: A caring and complex man

'Nothing matters, and everything matters,' Leonard once admitted, shedding light on his dual nature. Hard-working, politically engaged and obsessed with record-keeping, he nevertheless worried about the futility of life. In his autobiography, he confessed: 'I must have in a long life ground through between 150,000 and 200,000 hours of perfectly useless work.'

Leonard's attention to detail was compulsive. Despite a tremor in his hands, he wrote everything down. He was a bureaucrat at heart, recording all his expenses, details of Virginia's changing mental state, the gramophone records he acquired and exactly when he listened to them. And he made a point of always answering a letter on the day it arrived.

Political work

Leonard's years in Ceylon had persuaded him of the need to bring down the colonial system. Describing himself as 'a socialist of a peculiar sort', he condemned imperialism and capitalism, and believed in freedom, democracy, equality and justice. He became an advisor to the Labour Party and the Fabian Society, supported the co-operative movement and wrote political tracts and reports, one of which formed the basis for the League of Nations. His standing in the political world led to editorial positions with journals such as *The Nation*, the *Political Quarterly* (which he co-founded in 1931) and the *New Statesman*.

Writing

Despite writing numerous books on politics and a few works of fiction, Leonard is best remembered for his five-volume autobiography. Published in the last decade of his life, it sheds precious light on the development of the Bloomsbury Group and his life with Virginia.

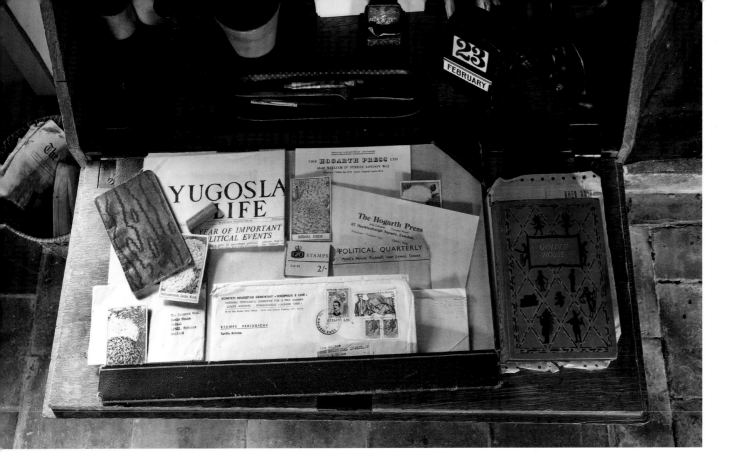

Looking after Virginia

Just a few months after marrying Virginia, Leonard was brought face to face with his wife's crippling condition. In September 1913, she tried to kill herself by taking an overdose of sleeping pills. Her stomach was pumped and, although she was brought back to physical health, the depression lasted on and off for three years. Leonard reacted with unfailing devotion. Realising how easily Virginia's nerves could be frayed, he prescribed a routine of quiet occupation and the avoidance of unnecessary stresses. He created the structure she needed to write and be creative. After 20 years of marriage, Virginia wrote in her diary, on 28 May 1931: 'If it were not for the divine goodness of L. how many times I should be thinking of death.'

Opposite A pensive Leonard, in his armchair at Monk's House, in 1931

Above Leonard's small desk in the Sitting Room displays items pertaining to his work as a publisher and journalist, and to his passion for plants

Animal lover

Leonard was always drawn to animals. He once owned a pet marmoset named Mitzi, who would perch on his shoulder for most of the day. He and Virginia always had dogs. On cold evenings, Mitzi and their spaniel Pinka would snuggle together in front of the fire at Monk's House. 'They were just sharing the house and garden together, and this respect was absolutely mutual,' Leonard wrote about his pets.

'Madness is terrific'

Virginia's depression plagued her repeatedly. Yet despite all the agony and setbacks, there was something to be gained from it. 'Madness is terrific I can assure you, and not to be sniffed at; and in its lava I still find most of the things I write about.'

In her essay *On Being Ill*, she describes how illness can bring a new form of awareness and how words take on a 'mystic quality' so that 'we grasp what is beyond their surface meaning'. Her prose would not have had the same depth of expression had she not suffered so much.

Moving to Richmond

Virginia's depressive episode after her marriage prompted a move from central London to the quiet suburb of Richmond. In March 1915, the couple leased Hogarth House, a large Georgian residence. Leonard loved it, describing it as 'the perfect envelope for ordinary life' – but there was nothing ordinary about their life at the time. Virginia was delusional, suffering from anxiety, insomnia and bouts of violence which four live-in nurses and specialist 'nerve doctors' tried to control. Slowly she recovered, her convalescence composed of simple tasks such as typing, cooking and gardening.

'In illness words seem to possess a mystic quality. We grasp what is beyond their surface meaning, gather instinctively this, that, and the other – a sound, a colour, here a stress, there a pause – which the poet, knowing words to be meagre in comparison with ideas, has strewn about his page to evoke, when collected, a state of mind which neither words can express nor the reason explain.'

Virginia Woolf, *On Being Ill*

Final words

Depression finally got the better of Virginia in 1941, as the full horror of the Second World War revealed itself. Following the bombing of the couple's London home and the deaths of a string of close friends and of her nephew Julian Bell, killed in the Spanish Civil War, Virginia felt the onset of another breakdown. On the morning of 28 March, she wrote her final letter to Leonard , in which she admitted: 'I feel certain that I am going mad again. I feel I can't go through another of those terrible times. And I shan't recover this time.' She then headed to the River Ouse, filled her coat pockets with stones and drowned herself.

Left Virginia at Monk's House in 1931, aged 49. By that time she had experienced many depressive episodes; most of these would severely debilitate her for months

Above The River Ouse near Monk's House, where Virginia drowned herself in March 1941

The Hogarth Press

Virginia and Leonard had always been interested in the craft of making books. Virginia had learned bookbinding as a young woman. Leonard believed the distraction of printing would help Virginia during her breakdowns and provide a pause from the intellectual effort of writing. Both liked the idea of publishing works by their friends.

So, in April 1917, when the couple noticed a small hand-press in a shop window, they immediately acquired it. Using the instruction booklet that came with the machine, they taught themselves how to print. 'We've been so absorbed in printing... I can hardly tear myself away to go to London, or see anyone,' Virginia wrote to her sister Vanessa in May of that year. Within three months, their first book was published: *Two Stories*, featuring *Three Jews* by Leonard and *The Mark on the Wall* by Virginia.

Virginia's story revealed her fresh approach to writing. The narrator, noticing a mark on the wall, ponders the mystery and impermanence of life, exposing the workings of the mind: consciousness becomes as important as external reality in this unusual tale. Writing it left Virginia exhilarated. 'I shall never forget the moment I wrote "The Mark on the Wall" – all in a flash, as if flying,' she recollected to her friend Ethel Smyth.

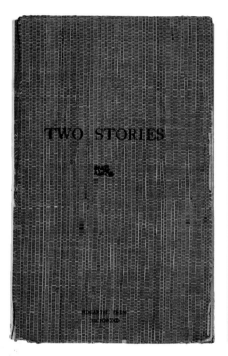

Above *Two Stories*, the first book produced by the fledgling Hogarth Press in 1917. The other book covers pictured here were all created by Vanessa Bell, whose designs helped create a recognisable brand for the Press

Success and more

The Hogarth Press was not a premeditated commercial success. Almost despite themselves, the couple created a flourishing enterprise. At the beginning, Virginia and Leonard hand-printed every book themselves. They focused on small, experimental texts and up-and-coming writers and thinkers, such as Katherine Mansfield, T.S. Eliot, E.M. Forster and Clive Bell. After four years, they acquired a larger press and started selling books directly to booksellers, rather

'How readily our thoughts swarm upon a new object, lifting it a little way, as ants carry a blade of straw so feverishly, and then leave it...'

Virginia Woolf,
The Mark on the Wall

than to friends and acquaintances and through subscriptions. Soon they were employing staff. The Press offered the couple, who would remain childless, the chance to work together on a creative outlet; it was a collaborative enterprise – a 'tremendous thing' such as Virginia had described in her pre-marriage letter to Leonard. Crucially, it gave Virginia the freedom to write exactly what she wanted, without pandering to editors and publishers. She was, she realised, 'the only woman in England free to write what I like'.

Collaborating with Vanessa
Virginia's sister, the artist Vanessa Bell, played a key role in developing a recognisable brand for the Hogarth Press. Her stylised duo-tone artwork appears on many of the Press's covers, including all but the first two of Virginia's books. Vanessa was also responsible for the company logo: the profile of a wolf's head, a visual pun on the name of its founders.

'Moments of being'

Virginia continued to test the limits of her craft. Published in 1919, *Kew Gardens* was another experimental short story. Its premise was simple yet utterly modern: the author follows four pairs of people – each in conversation – as they walk past a flower bed on a hot summer's day. Like an impressionist painting, the story flickers with light, colour and atmosphere capturing a deeply sensory reality.

Virginia's pioneering work on short stories paved the way for more adventurous novels, such as *Jacob's Room* (1922). In this rule-breaking character study, we experience the protagonist, Jacob Flanders, in a series of glimpses, often from the viewpoint of the women in his life. We get a shifting sense of who he is – a man composed of memories and impressions.

Throughout her life, Virginia challenged established ideas of identity and reality. She questioned the limits of human knowledge and yet brilliantly captured what she called 'moments of being': instants of intense awareness and beauty when one sees life clearly and powerfully.

'Nobody sees any one as he is, let alone an elderly lady sitting opposite a strange young man in a railway carriage. They see a whole – they see all sorts of things – they see themselves...'

Virginia Woolf, *Jacob's Room*

On writing

Virginia wrote passionately about the act of writing. In her diaries, she monitors her work's progress, anxiously questioning her objectives and revealing the painstaking process of putting words on paper. In her letters, she shares her thoughts with fellow writers and friends. And in a series of brilliant essays, such as *Modern Fiction, Character in Fiction* and *The New Biography*, she ponders the aims of contemporary literature.

A bestseller

Virginia dreaded critics' reaction to her work, but she needn't have worried about *Orlando* (1928). This celebration of her one-time lover and close friend Vita Sackville-West was an immediate success. The book is a swirling, sensuous adventure, wonderfully rich in evocative images. Here too Virginia broke established rules of biography, tracing the unrealistically long and gender-shifting life of aspiring writer and aristocrat, Orlando, as he progresses from the Elizabethan age to modern times, first as a man, then as a woman. Among its many themes are – again – notions of identity, and, importantly, what it means to be a woman. *Orlando* is now regarded as a key work in the canon of women's literature, as influential as Virginia's other great feminist work, *A Room of One's Own* (1929) (see pages 20–21).

Virginia the feminist

'A woman must have money and a room of her own if she is to write fiction,' Virginia famously wrote in *A Room of One's Own*. In this extended essay, she states that the reason why literature and history are male-dominated areas is not – as was widely believed at the time – because women are inferior. It is entirely due to circumstance, women being hindered by a social system which denies them financial independence and intellectual freedom.

In Virginia's day most women did not attend school and university, were excluded by law from inheriting, and were expected to marry, look after the home and have children. 'It is significant that of the four great women novelists – Jane Austen, Emily Brontë, Charlotte Brontë and George Eliot – not one of them had a child, and two were unmarried.' Interestingly, Virginia herself did not have children – a decision that seems to have been made mostly by Leonard, who was worried that bearing and raising a child would affect his wife's mental health.

In the essay Virginia goes on to explain how literature is dominated by male standards. And yet 'it is probable, however, that both in life and art the values of a woman are not the values of a man. Thus, when a woman comes to write a novel, she will find that she is perpetually wishing to alter established values – to make serious what appears insignificant to a man, and trivial what is to him important.'

Women's words

Virginia called for a new kind of writing unhindered by masculine precedent. 'Before a woman can write exactly as she wishes to write, she has many difficulties to face. To begin with, there is the technical difficulty – so simple apparently; in reality so baffling – that the very form of the sentence does not fit her. It is a sentence made by men; it is too loose, too heavy, too pompous for a woman's use.' Women writers, she believed, should create a new kind of sentence 'that takes the natural shape of her thought without crushing or distorting it.'

Killing the angel in the house

Virginia's most powerful feminist outcry appeared in her essay, *Professions for Women*. Referencing Coventry Patmore's poem, *The Angel in the House* (1862), which praises the qualities of the perfect wife such as meekness, patience and self-sacrifice, she thundered: 'I turned upon her and caught her by the throat. I did my best to kill her… Had I not killed her she would have killed me. She would have plucked the heart out of my writing.'

Opposite **Portrait of Virginia Woolf taken by Lenare in 1929, the same year she published *A Room of One's Own***

Below **Vanessa Bell's cover for *A Room of One's Own*, one of her most pared-down designs**

'Women have served all these centuries as looking glasses possessing the magic and delicious power of reflecting the figure of man at twice its natural size.'

Virginia Woolf,
A Room of One's Own

'Friendships with women interest me'

The death of her mother no doubt prompted Virginia to seek solace in close female friendships. Throughout her adult life she enjoyed relationships with women, many of whom shaped her life and her writing.

Vanessa Bell (1879–1961)

'Nobody except Leonard matters to me as you matter… and always I feel I'm writing more for you than for anybody,' Virginia told her sister. At times Virginia envied Vanessa's family life – she had three children – but both shared a passion for their respective art forms and supported the other, Vanessa when Virginia was unwell, and Virginia when Vanessa's son Julian was tragically killed in 1937, aged just 29.

Vita Sackville-West (1892–1962)

Vita Sackville-West, the famous gardener, writer and aristocratic grande dame of Sissinghurst, first met Virginia in 1922. 'At first you think she is plain, then a sort of spiritual beauty imposes itself on you… Darling, I have quite lost my heart,' Vita confessed to her husband Harold Nicolson, with whom she had a famously open marriage. Virginia wrote that Vita made her feel 'virgin, shy, & schoolgirly'. A few years later the women started a brief but passionate affair. This was followed by a profound friendship that lasted until Virginia's death. Both shared a common bond in writing and both – through their actions and their words – redefined what it meant to be a woman and a wife.

Violet Dickinson (1865–1948)

Seventeen years her senior, Violet Dickinson met Virginia when she was just a teenager. This motherly figure was exactly what the young and vulnerable Virginia, who had suffered so many losses, needed at the time. Violet nursed Virginia during her first breakdown and played a crucial role in encouraging her career, acting as a sounding board and introducing her to literary editors. When Virginia married Leonard, the women saw less of each other but they continued corresponding.

Katherine Mansfield (1888–1923)

'I was jealous of her writing – the only writing I have ever been jealous of,' Virginia admitted. The pair met in February 1917. At the time Virginia wanted to publish one of Katherine's short stories. They became friends, but it was a complicated and short-lived relationship. Although they admired each other's work and exchanged ideas about writing, Virginia was particularly sensitive to Katherine's criticism. Katherine, plagued by ill-health, succumbed to tuberculosis in 1923, aged just 34.

Ethel Smyth (1858–1944)

Ethel Smyth – composer, writer and suffragette – was Virginia's last great female friend. She had confessed to being in love with Virginia even before meeting her. When they did meet in 1930, the older woman, aged 71, became obsessed. She wrote streams of passionate letters. Virginia, who was entering her fifties, enjoyed being idolised. Ethel gave her a platform from which to write deeply autobiographical letters.

Life in Sussex

Even before they married, Virginia and Leonard spent time away from London, in a pretty Regency house at the foot of the South Downs.

This was Asheham House, which Vanessa and Virginia jointly leased in 1910. Leonard, then still just a friend, was one of the first visitors. As a married couple, he and Virginia virtually claimed Asheham as theirs. They had always enjoyed the South Downs – the undulating hills, vast skies and distant views of the sea – but now their affection blossomed into something stronger: a deep connection to place. When in 1916 Vanessa and her artist companion Duncan Grant moved to Charleston Farmhouse just seven miles away, this quiet area of East Sussex earned its place in both sisters' hearts. They would remain anchored to it for the rest of their lives.

Acquiring Monk's House
In 1918 Virginia and Leonard were given one year's notice to leave Asheham house. There was no doubt in their minds: they would have to find a new home nearby. Rashly, in June 1919 Virginia made an offer on a house in the centre of Lewes. She soon regretted her decision: what she and Leonard really wanted was a country retreat.

By chance they passed an auctioneers' notice for Monk's House in the unspoilt village of Rodmell, two miles from Lewes. The couple already knew the building from the outside, having walked past it on their regular walks in the Downs. It was a simple, weatherboarded house, on the edge of a narrow road leading out of the village towards fields. Its position and character were immediately appealing, and so the following afternoon Virginia cycled to Rodmell to have a look inside.

Despite its many drawbacks – the rooms were small, the kitchen damp, there was no electricity or mains water – Virginia was besotted. She sensed 'a profound pleasure at the size & shape & fertility & wildness of the garden'. She admired its 'infinity of fruitbearing trees' and the 'well kept rows of peas, artichokes, potatoes'. 'I could fancy a very pleasant walk in the orchard under the apple trees,' she wrote in her diary, 'with the grey extinguisher of the church steeple pointing my boundary.' Already she felt a sense of ownership. The garden was surprisingly large and right on the edge of seemingly endless meadows – and it was enveloped by the South Downs.

Hiding her excitement, Virginia described the house to Leonard 'as quietly as I could' and the pair went to see it together. Leonard was smitten too. The couple bid for it at auction on 1 July 1919 and acquired it for £700. They moved in on 1 September.

'We had often noticed the house and garden before 1919, for walking up and down the lane between Rodmell Church and the village street you could look over the wall into the orchard and garden and catch a glimpse of the back of the house.'

Leonard Woolf,
Beginning Again

Left The garden at
Monk's House in summer,
with its distinctive view of
Rodmell Church

Making a home

Virginia and Leonard set about making their new home as comfortable and attractive as they could. Having moved their furniture from Asheham and acquired a few items from the sale of the contents of Monk's House, Virginia started decorating.

She painted the walls in shades of blue, yellow, pomegranate and green. Unsure of her talent as a decorator, she asked Vanessa for advice. Her sister obliged and, with Duncan Grant, provided painted furniture, textiles and tiles, as well as paintings. Meanwhile, Leonard threw himself into the garden.

Improvements

The couple soon realised just how primitive their house really was. On their first night the kitchen flooded; they discovered that on rainy days water would drain down from the garden through the house. Mice scuttled across beds at night. In the winter the rooms were freezing. But as their wealth grew, Leonard and Virginia were able to make substantial changes. Royalties from books helped a considerable amount.

In 1927 Virginia proudly announced to Vita Sackville-West that she had acquired two WCs: 'one paid for by Mrs Dalloway, the other by The Common Reader'. This must have felt like a triumph. For years the couple had had to make

Above This side of the Sitting Room was for reading and sitting by the fire. The large armchair was one of Virginia's favourite seats; its cover features an abstract design by Vanessa Bell

Left Looking into the Sitting Room

Virginia was 'an untidy liver... her room tended to become not merely untidy but squalid.'

Leonard Woolf

'Ramshackle informality'

The house was a lot messier than it appears today. Books, magazines and newspapers were scattered about the place, on tables, chairs, floors, even clogging up the staircase. Dog and cat food was left in bowls around the house. Leonard recalled it as a house of 'ramshackle informality'.

do with an outside earth closet, jokingly referred to by Virginia as 'the romantic chamber'. In 1929, following the success of *Orlando*, the couple bought a new oil stove. In 1930, they transformed the attic into a study for Leonard and built a two-storey extension. One of the new rooms became Virginia's bedroom, quirkily accessed only from the outside; the other became a sitting room.

In 1931 electricity was installed, followed by a telephone line in 1932 and mains water in 1934. The erection of a new writing lodge in 1934 (see page 48) seemed to celebrate the end of a series of major improvements.

A home for art

Monk's House was never as overtly aesthetic as Vanessa's Charleston Farmhouse – this was a writers' not an artists' home after all – but it has charming Bloomsbury interiors nonetheless. Significantly, much of the art represents people and places that Virginia and Leonard knew and loved.

Personal connections

Filled with pictures, furniture and decorative pieces by Vanessa and Duncan, the rooms are also home to paintings by Bloomsbury artists, such as Roger Fry and Frederick Porter, art pottery by Vanessa's son, Quentin Bell, and delicate paintings by her daughter, Angelica Garnett.

In Virginia's bedroom, an oil painting by Duncan Grant shows a dramatic representation of *Monk's House Garden and St Peter's Church, Rodmell* (1923). In the Dining Room, Vanessa's portrait of her sister captures the author's melancholy nature; it was probably painted at Ashesham House in 1912, just before Virginia married Leonard. On the adjacent wall is *Leonard Woolf at a Window in Monk's House* (1950) by Trekkie Parsons (see page 62), Leonard's companion in later life. It shows him reading a paper, with a flowering plant, and pile of books and more newspapers – a painterly summary of his interests. In the Kitchen, Vanessa's small studies of Virginia and Leonard's spaniel, Sally, are particularly touching.

The influence of Post-Impressionism

Roger Fry brought the Post-Impressionists to the attention of the British public when he organised his landmark exhibition 'Manet and the Post-Impressionists' in 1910–11. When she saw the works of Van Gogh, Cézanne, Matisse, Gauguin and Picasso, Vanessa felt 'a sudden liberation and encouragement to feel for oneself which was absolutely overwhelming'. Like the Post-Impressionists, Bloomsbury artists experimented with colour, line and form. They wanted to convey a more expressive response to the external world than the Impressionists had achieved.

With its blocks of colour Roger Fry's *Landscape at Asheham House* (c.1913–9) shows the influence of Cézanne. So too does Vanessa Bell's *Apples* (c.1919). Cézanne himself had famously worked on still-lifes of apples in bowls, in which he deliberately skewed perspective and relied on shifting planes of colour.

Opposite (Clockwise from top left): *Apples* by Vanessa Bell, c.1918; *Leonard Woolf at a Window in Monk's House* by Trekkie Parsons, 1950; *Sally* by Vanessa Bell, 1939; *Landscape at Asheham House* by Roger Fry, c.1913–9; and *Monk's House Garden and St Peter's Church, Rodmell* by Duncan Grant, 1923

The brush and the pen

Virginia was fascinated by what contemporary artists were achieving at the time. Of Cézanne, she wrote: 'His pictures are so audaciously and provocatively content to be paint, that, the very pigment they say, seems to challenge us, to press on some nerve, to stimulate, excite.' Like him she challenged traditional means of representation. She used her pen as a paintbrush, paring away unnecessary detail, shedding light on what was 'beyond the visual'. She created works of literary art in which, like in a painting, everything is connected.

Daily life

Life at Monk's House revolved around a routine of work interspersed with periods of quiet occupation. Leonard and Virginia visited from London at weekends and stayed for longer spells in the summer months and during Easter and Christmas.

A typical day

Most days followed a set pattern. Leonard made breakfast at 8 o'clock and took it up to Virginia's bedroom (the couple always slept in separate rooms). Once she had looked at her post, Virginia read her previous day's work aloud in the bath. The cook, Louie Everett, working in the kitchen below, remembered: 'On and on she went, talk, talk, talk: asking questions and giving herself the answers. I thought there must be two or three people up there with her.' Leonard understood his wife's intentions, recalling: 'She always said the sentences out loud that she had written during the night. She needed to know if they sounded right and the bath was a good resonant place for trying them out.'

Then, if the weather was clement, Virginia went to her writing lodge across the garden and worked there for the rest of the morning. If it was too cold, she stayed in her bedroom. Leonard, meanwhile, retreated to his upstairs study overlooking the garden. Both would work until midday. 'Neither of us ever took a day's holiday unless we were too ill to work or unless we went away on a regular, as it were, authorised holiday,' Leonard wrote in his autobiography. 'We should have felt it to be not merely wrong but unpleasant not to work every morning for seven days a week and for about 11 months a year.'

After a simple lunch, it was time for an hour or so of reading, after which the couple went for a walk in the Downs or did some gardening. Tea, taken at four o'clock, was usually combined with letter- and diary-writing. After supper the couple sat in the sitting room, reading and listening to music on the gramophone.

Visitors

Leonard and Virginia guarded their privacy very closely and only invited close friends and family to Monk's House. Vanessa Bell, Duncan Grant, Lytton Strachey, T.S. Eliot, Vita Sackville-West, E.M. Forster and Ethel Smyth were regular visitors. They would play bowls on the back lawn, relax in deck chairs by the writing lodge, and talk at length, much as they had done in Bloomsbury. Although she loved her friends, Virginia admitted that: 'The truth is, I like it when people actually come; but I love it when they go.'

Right Angelica Garnett, Vanessa Bell, Clive Bell, Virginia Woolf and Maynard Keynes outside the Writing Lodge in 1935

Opposite Virginia reading in one of the upstairs rooms at Monk's House, date unknown

Exploring Monk's House

Monk's House radiates a quiet beauty that reflects the personalities of Leonard and Virginia.

The Sitting Room

In 1926, the Woolfs knocked down a partition wall to create this large room. Relaxed and intimate, it combines areas for reading, writing and eating. The furniture, ranging from the 17th to the 20th centuries, is an eclectic mix of inherited, antique and contemporary items.

Dotted around are pieces by Vanessa and Duncan. The dining table and four chairs were painted by the pair in the early 1930s. The table top bears a geometric motif with criss-cross strokes, similar to those found on some of Vanessa's book cover designs, while the backs of the chairs bear Virginia Woolf's painted monogram.

The square coffee table in the centre of the room, another piece from the early 1930s, is topped with tiles by Duncan Grant depicting Venus at her toilet. While the subject matter is traditional and the use of yellow and blue a nod to ceramic heritage, the treatment, relying on informal brushstrokes, is utterly modern.

The firescreen, with its canvas-work still-life, was executed by Duncan's mother, Mrs Ethel Bartle Grant, to his own design. Next to it, the upholstered armchair was one of Virginia's favourite reading chairs. Its cover features a print of Vanessa's 'Abstract' pattern which she designed for Alan Walton Textiles. Vanessa's love of shape and colour lent itself particularly well to pattern design.

What happens upstairs?

Sadly the upstairs rooms are not open to the public as the house is still lived in for security reasons. In the Woolfs' time there were five rooms: Leonard's bedroom, a small spare bedroom above the dining room, a bathroom above the kitchen, and an upstairs sitting room above Virginia's bedroom. Leonard also had part of the attic converted into his study.

The Omega Workshops

The table-and-chairs set in the dining room is stylistically similar to pieces made for the Omega Workshops – a commercial venture set up by Roger Fry with Vanessa and Duncan in 1913. Their aim was to give expression to Bloomsbury artists through decorative pieces and interiors. Roger Fry explained his intentions thus: 'It is time that the spirit of fun was introduced into furniture and fabrics. We have suffered too long from the dull, and the stupidly serious.' The workshops produced a vast range of items, from lamps, rugs, carpets, screens and furniture to jewellery, cushions, scarves, wall hangings, tiles, pottery, boxes, fans and parasols. Never a financial success, they closed in 1919, but had a strong influence on interior decoration in the 1920s.

Left This Sitting Room contains many pieces of fine and decorative arts created for, or acquired by, the couple

Music

Leonard loved music, as evidenced by his elegant 1920s EMG radio-gramophone on the back wall. He was particularly fond of Mozart's piano concertos, Bach's chamber music and Beethoven's quartets, and also enjoyed Haydn and Schubert. As well as listening to records, the couple would also tune in to live concerts on the radio.

Despite not being musical herself, Virginia had enjoyed listening to music from an early age. Like painting, it influenced her writing. Its rhythm and harmonies affected her prose and the structure of her books, as she pointed out to her friend Elizabeth Trevelyan in 1940: 'Its odd, for I'm not regularly musical, but I always think of my books as music before I write them.' In the letter she compares the act of writing her biography of Roger Fry to composing music:

'There was such a mass of detail that the only way I could hold it together was by abstracting it into themes. I did try to state them in the first chapter, and then to bring in developments and variations, and then to make them all heard together and end by bringing back the first theme in the last chapter.'

Books everywhere

Books dominated the house. The painted pine bookcase and the scattered tomes on the coffee table in the sitting room hint at the couple's passion for reading. After Leonard's death all the books at Monk's House were sold off. You can see the full inventory of the couple's library – over 6,000 items – in Virginia's bedroom. The collection is now held at Washington State University; it includes one of the most complete sets of Hogarth Press books in existence.

Left A corner of the
Sitting Room

'Few people ask from books what books can give us.'

Virginia Woolf,
How Should One Read a Book?

On reading

In 1925 Virginia wrote a short essay in which she ponders: *How Should One Read a Book?* Her answer is straightforward: let go of expectations, follow your instincts and draw your own conclusions. Crucially, 'do not dictate to your author, try to become him. Be his fellow worker and accomplice.' Virginia gives in to moments of lyricism as she delights in the joys of fiction, poetry and biography. Her essay is an ode to reading – the one thing she enjoyed as much as writing.

The Dining Room

Oddly situated just as you enter the house, the dining room was created in 1926 when a dividing wall was taken down. The Woolfs had previously used this space as a bedroom (see page 40).

The sunken part of the dining room is dominated by a table and six painted chairs from 1933. Designed by Vanessa Bell, the needlework panels on the chair backs depict bowls of flowers against a window. These, along with the large mirror in the room, were embroidered by Duncan Grant's mother. On 28 December 1937, Virginia wrote to thank her for the mirror, a Christmas present: 'I can't tell you what a joy – quite undeserved though – your embroidery is to me. It hangs on a chair back at this moment, but no dog or cat or human is allowed to sit on it. I don't think though that you ought to give such sumptuous presents… It is exquisitely lovely.'

Playing bowls

Under the stairs are Leonard and Virginia's original bowling woods. Both loved the game and were highly competitive. You can enjoy a game too: a set of bowls is available on the lawn.

Right The Dining Room features a few ceramics by Vanessa Bell's son Quentin, including the lamp in the corner and the bowl on the table

Far right *Quentin Bell Reading* by Vanessa Bell, c.1936–8

A talented nephew

The Dining Room features charming pieces of art pottery by Vanessa's son Quentin Bell: a lamp, made especially for Monk's House in 1982, and a bowl with pink and blue scroll brushstrokes. Both items, along with his other ceramic works in the house, display the influence of – and beautifully complement – the earlier Bloomsbury pieces by Vanessa and Duncan.

Despite his artistic abilities (he also painted), Quentin was most famous for his academic achievements. He became a professor of art history and wrote books on the Bloomsbury Group and Charleston. Shortly before his death, Leonard asked his nephew to write Virginia's biography and gave him access to all her private diaries and papers. Quentin's two-volume *Virginia Woolf: A Biography* (1972) is still considered a key work, combining psychological insight and uniquely intimate perspective. You can see his portrait, by Vanessa, in the Sitting Room.

Vita's visits

When the dining room was still a bedroom, Vita Sackville-West used it as a guest. Her love affair with Virginia probably started in 1926, when she stayed at Monk's House while Leonard was away in London. Although Virginia never confirmed the physical nature of their relationship, Vita, never coy about matters of the flesh, wrote to her own husband: 'and I did sleep with her at Rodmell'. In a passionate letter of 1926, Virginia declared: 'Look here Vita — throw over your man, and we'll go to Hampton Court and dine on the river together and walk in the garden in the moonlight and come home late and have a bottle of wine and get tipsy, and I'll tell you all the things I have in my head, millions, myriads…'

Vita and Virginia met several times at Monk's House and at Sissinghurst. Leonard was aware of their intimacy and let the affair, which lasted a couple of years, run its course. Virginia declared in her diary of that year: 'The truth is one has room for a good many relationships.'

Above Virginia and Vita in the garden at Monk's House in 1933

Portraits of Leonard and Virginia

The Dining Room is home to expressive portraits of Leonard and Virginia.

1 Vanessa painted this preliminary sketch in 1933–4 and gave it to her sister for Christmas in 1935. It shows Virginia seated in an armchair at 52 Tavistock Square, her London home at the time. With a few loose brushstrokes Vanessa creates a subtly expressive portrait: despite the lack of facial features, the pose, simple clothes and hairstyle mark out the sitter, surrounded by books and bookshelves, as Virginia Woolf and no one else. The finished painting sits in Vanessa's bedroom at Charleston.

2 This oil portrait, again by Vanessa, dates from 1912. It depicts a pensive Virginia with arms folded on a table, possibly her desk, in similar dress and pose to a portrait by Roger Fry which was probably painted at the same time.

3&4 Leonard's companion in later life was the artist and engraver Trekkie Parsons. Monk's House is home to many of her paintings, including these two evocative oil portraits of Leonard. *Leonard Woolf in Doorway* (*c*.1950) shows him holding a bunch of flowers in front of the door in Virginia's bedroom. While a stream of sunshine brightens the room, the open door reveals a light-infused garden. *Portrait of Leonard* (*c*.1950–69) is a more traditional head-and-shoulder treatment of the genre; he is deep in thought, looking down with his temple resting on his right hand.

Previous owners

The picture above the mantelpiece in the dining room holds a key to the story of the house, a subject which fascinated Leonard. It is thought to represent the Glazebrook family, who lived at Monk's House in the 19th century.

This portrait is one of three paintings (the other two are in the kitchen) bought by Leonard when the contents of the house were auctioned off in 1919. Both Leonard and Virginia liked their primitive style and loved the idea that these 'inherited' items connected them to the history of their home.

'Their spirits, I almost felt and feel, walk in the house clattering up and down the narrow stairs, now deeply worn by the countless comings and goings of Clears, Glazebrooks and Verralls... And once when a floorboard was taken up by a workman we found a tiny little wooden eighteenth century shoe; another time I found in the cellar a George III four-penny piece which appeared to have been charred in a fire.'

Leonard Woolf, writing about the previous owners of Monk's House

Right The mantelpiece in the Dining Room, with one of the Glazebrook paintings (c.1830–50) above

A potted history of Monk's House

By researching the deeds of the house, Leonard was able to trace its history. In the late 17th century John de la Chambre, owner of Hall Place in Rodmell, commissioned the building of Monk's House, a three-unit cottage, to house members of his staff. (Hall Place was on the site of Charnes Cottage which stands next to Monk's House today.)

The Clears

In 1707 John Clear or Cleere, a carpenter, acquired Monk's House from John de la Chambre. It remained in the family until 1796 when it was sold to John Glazebrook, who owned the mill on the Down behind the village. According to Leonard, the house was known as Clears at the time.

The Glazebrooks

John Glazebrook married Sarah Ellis with whom he had three sons. The family were apparently self-sufficient: the Woolfs found evidence in the garden of a pig house, hen house and granary machinery. When John died in 1826, his son William, aged 21, moved into Monk's House and took over the mill. In the mid-19th century his brother John was the baker in the village, and also opened the post office in 1861. In 1877 William died from typhoid aged 71 and the house was sold to Jacob Verrall.

Right *A Woman by a Window* (probably Mercy Glazebrook), c.1830–50

The Verralls

Jacob Verrall is described in the Rodmell Vestry Minute Book in 1882 as a 'Surveyor of Highways, Assessor and Collector of Taxes and Overseer of the Poor'. In 1910, aged 66, he married Lydia Baker from Rodmell. She died suddenly in 1912; Jacob, distraught, started to suffer from anorexia nervosa. He died in 1919, having never fully recovered from the death of his wife.

Why Monk's House?

It is unlikely that the house was ever connected with the Church. Some have suggested that the name was an estate agent's invention. Others believe it was named after Jacob Verrall's previous property at Monk's Gate in Horsham.

The Kitchen

The Kitchen was chiefly the domain of the cook and housekeeper. Virginia didn't enjoy employing servants, but she couldn't do without them: cleaning and cooking meant time away from writing.

Virginia struggled to treat her staff autocratically and her more familiar relationship with them led to frequent arguments. She even quarrelled with Leonard about how to treat them. 'It is an absurdity, how much time L. & I have wasted in talking about servants,' she confessed in her diary in April 1929.

The couple employed two servants – cook Nelly Boxall and housekeeper Lottie Hope – whom they had brought down from London. In 1934, a local girl, Louie Everett, replaced Nelly; she remained working for Leonard until his death in 1969. She recalls her first days there: 'Mr Woolf explained their day was very carefully planned, almost hour by hour and it was important nothing should happen that could alter their routine.'

Dreaming of self-sufficiency

Virginia loved the idea of being servant-free. The addition of modern conveniences, such as a new stove in 1929, represented a kind of liberation: 'At this moment it is cooking my dinner in glass dishes perfectly I hope, without smell, waste or confusion; one turns handles, there is a thermometer. And so I see myself freer, more independent – & all one's life is a struggle for freedom – able to come down here with a chop in a bag & live on my own.' Virginia would

also indulge in making bread, cakes and jam, and bottling fruit from the garden. But, ever conscious of her duty as a writer, she sometimes regretted it afterwards, seeing it as a waste of time!

More ceramics

In the cabinet is a display of Bloomsbury china: cups and saucers by Quentin Bell, Wedgwood creamware pottery decorated by Vanessa and Duncan, a rare deep-blue Omega Workshops plate, and pieces of Vanessa's 1934 blue-and-white dinner service designed for Clarice Cliff.

Behind the screen

The part of the Kitchen you see today is the one which was there in 1919 when the Woolfs moved in. In 1920 the room was extended into a former coal store; this area is now a modern kitchen used by live-in staff. It is partitioned off by a bold 1980s screen by Angelica Garnett, Vanessa's daughter.

A home for pets

The dog baskets and dog portraits in this room are a reminder of how much Leonard and Virginia loved their pets – Sally the spaniel (pictured in this room), Nigg and Belle the sheepdogs, Sappho the cat and others all lived happily at Monk's House over the years. Virginia may have been inspired by experiences with her own pets when she wrote *Flush: A Biography*, in which she playfully looks at the life of Elizabeth Barrett Browning through the eyes of the poet's pet spaniel.

Left The Kitchen was basic and prone to flooding, but Virginia enjoyed spending time there; baking bread and bottling fruit were favourite, if distracting, pastimes

Virginia's Bedroom

Virginia was working on _A Room of One's Own_ when the extension to the house was being built in 1929. What she got was very much a room of her own. Inaccessible from the main house – you have to enter it from the garden – her new room provided perfect seclusion.

Virginia called it her 'airy bedroom'. Morning sunshine would stream into the room with its glorious views of the garden. By her bed she kept a pen and paper so that during her many restless nights, she could write.

'Sometimes it seemed as though she had had very little sleep,' Louie Everett recalled. 'These pieces of paper, some of them containing the same sentence over and over again would be in heaps about the room. They were on chairs, on the table and sometimes on the floor. It was Mrs Woolf's habit when she was working to leave her writing about in little heaps of paper. I would find them in the house too: in the sitting room and dining room, on the table and mantelpieces.'

Right Throughout their married life, Virginia and Leonard had separate bedrooms: Leonard slept upstairs, Virginia in the extension

Memories of St Ives

The fireplace tiles were a gift from Vanessa, as shown by the inscription in the left-hand floor tile: 'VW from VB 1930.' The central design represents a ship with a lighthouse in the distance, bringing to mind Virginia's book *To the Lighthouse*, published three years earlier, as well as the two other titles in what became known as her 'St Ives trilogy': *Jacob's Room* and *The Waves*.

The tiles are thought to represent Godrevy Island and lighthouse in St Ives Bay, Cornwall. This certainly seems possible, as the sisters spent many long and happy family holidays at Talland House near St Ives. According to Virginia's biographer Hermione Lee, 'Talland House became, in Virginia Woolf's imagination… something more than just a large square building near the sea in Cornwall. It is where she sites, for the whole of her life, the idea of happiness.'

In *Moments of Being,* Virginia describes in one essay her earliest memory there: 'If life has a base that it stands upon, if it is a bowl that one fills and fills and fills – then my bowl without a doubt stands upon this memory. It is of lying half asleep, half awake, in bed in the nursery at St Ives. It is of hearing the waves breaking, one, two, one, two, and sending a splash of water over the beach; and the breaking, one, two, one, two, behind a yellow blind. It is of hearing the blind draw its little acorn across the floor as the wind blew the blind out. It is of lying and hearing this splash and seeing this light, and feeling, it is almost impossible that I should be here; of feeling the purest ecstasy I can conceive.'

Virginia and fashion

Draped on the armchair is a delicate 1920s Chinese embroidered shawl – a gift to Virginia from her friend, the society hostess and patron of the arts, Lady Ottoline Morrell. It evokes a stylish Virginia, but this is not entirely correct.

Virginia often felt awkward about the way she looked, and she tended to wear dark colours and plain garments. Friends and witnesses recall her as nondescript and lacking ornament. In the 1920s, *Vogue* fashion editor Madge Garland, after seeing Virginia for the first time, wrote: 'There sat this beautiful and distinguished woman wearing what could only be described as an upturned wastepaper basket [on her head]'.

A cure for headaches

The slim bookcase by the armchair holds 39 Arden editions of Shakespeare owned by Virginia, which she hand-covered herself in 1936. Like printing, Virginia used book-binding as form of therapy. She found it particularly good for the treatment of headaches, from which she suffered all her life.

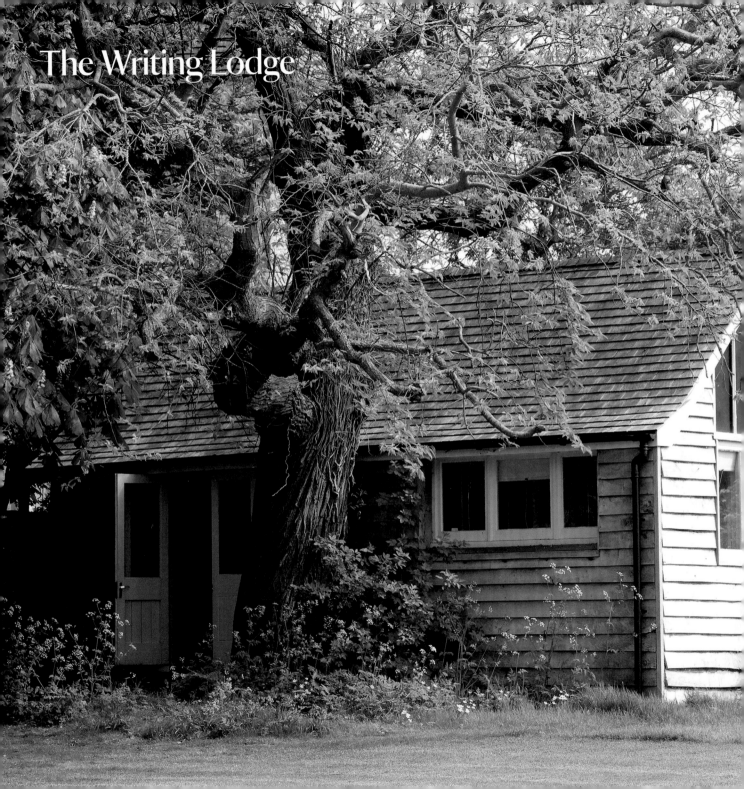

The Writing Lodge

In 1921 the Woolfs converted an old tool-shed in the garden into a writing room for Virginia. They added windows, and later a stove, so that she could work there in relative comfort.

Despite its lovely views towards the orchard, the space was far from ideal. The room above was used for storing apples and Leonard's frequent clattering upstairs proved a distraction.

By 1934 the couple had enough funds to build a new writing lodge. Delighted, Virginia wrote in her diary: 'My Lodge is demolished, the new house in process of building in the orchard. There will be open doors in front; & a view right over to Caburn. I think I shall sleep there on summer nights.' By December it was finished. Nestled in a corner of the garden under a tree, it was a simple yet attractive weatherboarded building with French windows and a little brick patio, which became a favoured spot for gatherings of friends. Here they would sit on deck chairs, admire the views of the Downs and watch highly competitive games of bowls. Meanwhile, during the day, Virginia enjoyed the solitude of her new writing space.

Inside the lodge

On the table are Virginia's tortoiseshell glasses and the folders, with handwritten labels, which she used for her manuscripts. Don't be fooled by the neatness. In Virginia's day the lodge would have been littered with pen nibs, scraps of paper and cigarette ends.

Creating more space

After Virginia's death Leonard extended the lodge for his companion Trekkie Parsons, who used the new space as an art studio. This area is now an exhibition room displaying photographs from the Monk's House albums – five volumes of photos taken by the Woolfs – portraying guests such as T.S. Eliot, John Maynard Keynes and E.M. Forster, Vanessa Bell and Duncan Grant.

The quirks of a writer

Virginia did not usually write at a table. Instead she sat in an armchair with a plywood board across her knees. On the board was attached a tray for pens and ink – an ingenious contraption which meant she never had to get up to replenish supplies and break the flow of her writing. Virginia liked using different-coloured inks – greens, blues and purples. Purple, her favourite, was reserved for letters. Later in the day she sat at her desk to type up and edit her morning's work.

Left The entrance on the right gives access to the studio, created for Trekkie Parsons in the 1950s

Above Virginia entered her lodge via these French windows

'The pride of our hearts'

Although the garden was Leonard's passion, Virginia got immense pleasure and inspiration from it.

Announcing her purchase of Monk's House to a friend in 1919, she wrote: 'The point of it is the garden… This is going to be the pride of our hearts; I warn you.' She was right. From the outset, Leonard was obsessed with his garden. He designed it, planted it and kept adding to it for the rest of his life. And Virginia enjoyed assisting him. Like walking, which she loved, simple gardening tasks – weeding, fruit picking, dead-heading – proved the ideal counterpoint to hours spent writing. The garden cast a spell on her, and its beauty stimulated lyrical descriptions.

As early as 1920 Leonard was planning flower beds and, according to Virginia, 'entirely remaking the garden'. It featured a few small, crumbling buildings, including an old laundry and earth closet. These were soon torn down, but Leonard kept the wall of the former granary, which, along with established trees, provided the perfect support for climbing plants such as wisteria, roses, clematis and trained fruit trees. He then created a network of narrow paths. These marked out the plan for the central and most ornamental part of the garden: a series of small enclosures, each with its own identity.

This idea was very much in keeping with the Arts and Crafts concept of garden rooms. The most shining example of this style is of course Sissinghurst, the garden of their friends Harold Nicolson and Vita Sackville-West. But whereas Sissinghurst is self-assured and dazzling, the garden at Monk's House possesses a quiet, introspective beauty, entirely fitting for two great thinkers.

Opposite Leonard in the garden, August 1931; note the red hot pokers behind him

Left The Flower Walk in summer, edged with lady's mantle (*Alchemilla mollis*), hardy geraniums and blue irises

A fruitful plot
One of the chief attractions of the garden was its productivity. The orchard yielded huge crops of plums, apples and pears, while the kitchen garden offered up a surplus of potatoes, cabbages, parsnips, carrots and onions. Unable to consume it all, the Woolfs sold their excess stock at the Lewes Women's Institute market – Leonard would cycle into the town with full baskets – or delighted their friends with gifts of fruit and vegetables.

Leonard's gardening style

Leonard was fond of bright colours, perhaps a result of having lived in Ceylon in his twenties. His favourite flowers – zinnias, dahlias, kniphofias and roses – offered him a palette of strong hues with which to paint his garden. But, ever the plantsman, he also liked white flowers, such as lilies and Japanese anemones.

Leonard bought flowers for their individual qualities. Rather than planting great clumps of one plant, he positioned one type next to another, creating – at times subtle, at times dazzling – colour combinations. In her diary, Virginia described it thus: 'Our garden is a perfect variegated chintz: asters, plumasters, zinnias, geums, nasturtiums & so on: all bright, cut from coloured papers, stiff, upstanding as flowers should be.'

Today's garden offers striking juxtapositions of deep purples and bright oranges, blues and reds, lilac blues and burnt oranges. At other times, pastel arrangements of lavender hues and pale pinks and purples create a more romantic effect.

Right The Millstone Terrace bursts into colour in summer with zinnias, crocosmias, *Perovskia* 'Blue Spire', campanulas and white echinaceas

Clockwise from far left A tapestry of flowers combining bright-yellow lysimachia, lavender-blue *Salvia* x *sylvestris* 'Mainacht', verbascums and roses; old-fashioned pale-pink roses and geraniums; tufted *Monarda* 'Cambridge Scarlet' framed by pink-and-white cranesbill geranium and *Campanula trachelium*; Michaelmas daisies and goldenrod; white echinaceas and cosmos

A tour of the garden

The Italian Garden

Shady, formal and minimal in its planting, the Italian Garden is unlike any other part of the garden. Its creation was inspired by a holiday in Tuscany in 1933. Virginia, practical and money-conscious as she was, bought the Italian-looking pots and statues from a grocer's shop in nearby Barcombe. The effect is simple yet evocative.

Hothouse flowers

Leonard had a passion for exotics. He grew cinerarias, begonias and gloxinias for the house and kept three heated greenhouses in the orchard. Virginia jokingly described them as his 'Crystal Palaces'. In one of these he focused entirely on growing cacti. In the 1950s Leonard added the lean-to conservatory to the house. It proved the ideal space in which to grow tender plants in his later years. It is still home to exotic and Mediterranean plants, including brugmansia, bougainvillea, yucca and oleander.

Right Abundant white phlox and goldenrod frame the path in the Flower Walk at the end of summer

Bottom right The Piggery Pond Garden

The Flower Walk

Two long and deep mixed borders frame a long brick path running from the steps by the house to the orchard. Roses, hydrangeas, magnolias and philadelphus are underplanted with spring bulbs, such as tulips, narcissi and fritillaria. In summer and early autumn, the beds overflow with herbaceous perennials – hardy geraniums, poppies, lilies, crocosmias, asters, phlox and Japanese anemones – creating a frothy cottage-garden effect.

The Millstone Terrace

Its name comes from the millstones which the Woolfs found in the garden – remnants from the Glazebrooks' mill. Leonard incorporated these into the paving in this area and also into his network of paths. He loved the thought that he was including bits of history into his garden. The large terracotta jars act as punctuation marks in the design.

The Piggery Pond Garden

Leonard loved ponds – he eventually had three in the garden. He and Virginia would spend hours watching the fish together. 'It is our passion to observe the gold fish,' Virginia wrote to a friend in 1931. 'There should be four, and one carp; but it is the rarest event to see them all together – and yet I can assure you that to see them matters more to us both than all that is said at the Hague.' If one of the fish was poorly, Leonard would bring it indoors and look after it in the fish tank in the Sitting Room until it had regained its strength.

In this area you will also find the bust of Virginia (1931) by sculptor Stephen Tomlin. Virginia hated sitting for it – so much so that the sculpture was left unfinished. The model in the garden is a copy; the plaster original does not survive.

The Fig Tree Garden

Brick floors and low flint walls mark this area of the garden, named after an ancient fig tree which already existed when Leonard and Virginia moved in. The slightly raised part at the back of this area marks the footprint of Virginia's first writing room. Now in its place stands a wonderful *Magnolia* x *soulangeana* 'Lennei' which has very unusual and colourful fruit in the autumn.

The Orchard

Relaxed and informal, the orchard was one of Virginia and Leonard's favourite parts of the garden, the 'very place to sit and talk for hours'. It probably inspired her short story, *In the Orchard*.

Leonard was as passionate about his orchard as he was about his ornamental garden. In his first winter at Monk's House, he bravely pruned the fruit trees in the freezing cold. Pruning was, to him, 'the pleasantest of occupations'. In 1927, he added some beehives to the orchard – Virginia was delighted, describing herself as a 'very bear where honey is concerned'. Leonard eventually became an expert beekeeper, and Virginia delighted in bottling the honey with him.

Above The Orchard in bloom; this productive and beautiful spot was much-loved by Leonard and Virginia

The Terrace Lawn

Leonard, keen to protect the views from his garden, acquired a field adjoining Monk's House in 1928, and created a large lawned area, dotted with yew trees, pampas grass, Lombardy poplars and a few other shrubs. Here the couple and their friends would enjoy congenial yet competitive games of bowls.

This also became the site of Leonard's third pond – a round, shallow body of water inspired by the dew ponds found on the Sussex Downs. Just beyond it were two elm trees, which the couple named Leonard and Virginia. Sadly these are now gone.

With the acquisition of this extra land, Leonard realised he needed help in the garden and so he appointed a full-time gardener, Percy Bartholomew, to assist him. Leonard bought a cottage in the village – 1 Park Cottages – for Percy and his family. Both men worked together in the garden for nearly 20 years; it was a fractious yet fruitful relationship, with frequent arguments and a few threats of dismissal and of resignation!

Defining happiness

Virginia once asked: 'What do you think is probably the happiest moment in one's whole life?' She answered the question herself: 'I think it's the moment when one is walking in one's garden, perhaps picking off a few dead flowers, and then suddenly one thinks: My husband lives in that house – and he loves me.' There is no doubt that the garden at Monk's House helped nurture their relationship.

Left *The Pond, Monk's House Garden, Rodmell* by Vanessa Bell, *c.*1935

Above The round pond on the Terrace Lawn was inspired by the dew ponds found on the Sussex Downs

Village life

Rodmell was a busy little community, with a pub, mill, forge, shop, bakery, cricket pitch, church and school. Its comings and goings were sometimes a source of nuisance to the quiet couple, but in later years Leonard and Virginia become increasingly drawn to its charms.

The school was right next to the house and Leonard would despair when the children stole apples from his orchard. Virginia felt equally annoyed by the noise from the playground. She also disliked the ringing of the nearby church bells – 'intermittent, sullen, didactic' – and any intrusion from villagers. All of this disturbed the peace she so needed for writing.

However, as the years went by, the couple became attached to the characters in the village and increasingly involved in its affairs. In 1940 Virginia announced to her friend Margaret Llewelyn Davies: 'I'm becoming, you'll be amused to hear, an active member of the Women's Institute, who've just asked me to write a play for the villagers to act.' Later in life Leonard became a governor of the school, helped with the Cricket Club and founded the Rodmell Horticultural Society. Its annual prize is still named after him.

War breaks out and depression sets in

When their London flat was bombed in 1940, Leonard and Virginia moved permanently to Rodmell. With the anti-Jewish threat rising, the couple plotted to commit suicide in their garage if Hitler invaded. Virginia's mental health took a battering and by early 1941 she was once again deeply depressed. Feeling worthless, she turned to housework and chores for distraction.

Her tactics proved insufficient, however. On 28 March, at one o'clock, Leonard went into the upstairs sitting room to listen to the news on the radio. Here he found Virginia's two letters (one for him and one for Vanessa). He ran to the river but could only find her walking stick. It was not until three weeks later that her body was spotted in the water by three teenagers on a cycling trip.

Virginia was cremated in Brighton, to the sound of 'Dance of the Blessed Spirits' by Christoph Willibald Gluck. Leonard buried her ashes under one of the two elm trees in the garden and marked the spot with a stone tablet engraved with the last lines from *The Waves*: 'Against you I fling myself, unvanquished and unyielding, O Death! The waves crashed on the shore.'

'They said: "Come to tea and let us comfort you" but it's no good. One must be crucified on one's own private cross… I know that V will not come across the garden from the Lodge and yet I look in that direction for her. I know that she has drowned and yet I listen for her to come in at the door.'

Note found amongst Leonard's personal papers after his death

Left **The Vegetable Garden in summer with sweet peas and poppies in full bloom**

Far left **The village of Rodmell**

Right **The two elms in the garden, which the couple named Leonard and Virginia**

After Virginia

Shortly after Virginia's death, Leonard fell in love with the artist Trekkie Parsons. His twilight years were made golden by this unusual yet happy relationship.

Despite being happily married, Trekkie embarked on a romantic relationship with Leonard in 1943. They had many things in common: a love of animals, books and art but, more importantly, a passion for gardening and exotic plants. This shared love was cemented in the garden at Monk's House, where they worked together for the next 25 years.

Trekkie, who never divorced her husband, enjoyed an unconventional double life. She spent weekdays in Sussex with Leonard and the weekend in London with her publisher husband Ian Parsons, who was well aware of the arrangement. Her time at Monk's House was spent not just gardening but painting, in her studio – christened the Blue Ark – which Leonard had created by extending Virginia's writing lodge in 1949.

Right Leonard outside his house in the 1950s

After Leonard

In 1969, aged 89, Leonard became seriously ill and on 14 August he suffered a fatal stroke. His ashes were buried alongside Virginia's beneath one of the elm trees. Shortly after his death, Leonard's nephew Quentin Bell wrote to Trekkie: 'I have never been quite sure whether you realised how grateful Vanessa was to you for taking Leonard out of that appalling misery and into a long and lovely autumn… I think you ought to know it.'

Leonard left Monk's House to Trekkie but in 1972, unable to live there without him, she offered to sell it to Sussex University. The purchase of Monk's House was her stipulation for gifting to the institution all the papers – both Leonard's and Virginia's – it contained. The deal proved unsatisfactory for the house: leased to academics over the summer, it was not adequately cared for and the garden became neglected.

Realising its potential demise, Nigel Nicolson, son of Vita Sackville-West and a frequent visitor in Virginia's time, wrote a plea to the National Trust in 1975: 'I am sure that V will come to be regarded… much as we regard Jane Austen or the Brontës and future generations would not forgive us if we allowed MH to be much altered. But unless something is done soon I fear this may happen.' Thanks to Nigel's commitment, Monk's House was saved and came into National Trust hands in 1981.

Top right Trekkie in one of Leonard's glasshouses at Monk's House

Right *The Garden Statue (Donatello's David)* by Trekkie Parsons, c.1950

'Life is a luminous halo'

Depression robbed Virginia of old age, but her spirit is still very much alive at Monk's House.

It is in the accumulation of small things that you will find it, and in the atmosphere of quiet domesticity that she and Leonard shared here for so many years.

Leonard knew well the soothing effect that Monk's House had on his wife. It was 'crucial for the stabilising of her mind and health and for her work'. It was in the day-to-day, the routine, the almost mundane, that Virginia's brilliantly creative mind could be free to explore and invent.

And it was in this habitual world – a world composed of writing, walking, reading and uncomplicated tasks – that she experienced perhaps her deepest happiness. Monk's House, with its 'ramshackle informality', is a testament, surely, to the simple life. A life where she could enjoy, as she wrote in her diary in 1932, 'a good week end at Rodmell – a week end of no talking, sinking at once into deep safe book reading; & then sleep: clear transparent; with the may tree like a breaking wave outside; & all the garden green tunnels, mounds of green: & then to wake into the hot still day, & never a person to be seen, never an interruption: the place to ourselves: the long hours.'

Below Taken from the balcony of Leonard's attic studio, this vista shows most of the beautifully rambling garden with its network of brick paths and old walls, and the spire of St Peter's Church an ever-present beacon